# silly Millies

# It Takes Three

Linda Hayward

Illustrations by
Robin Michal Koontz

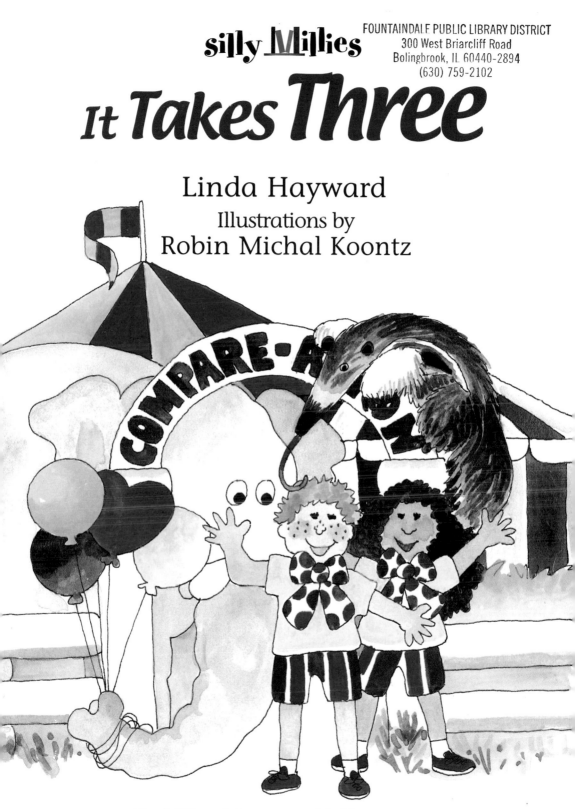

The Millbrook Press    Brookfield, Connecticut

*For Kelsey—L.H.*

Reading Consultant: Dr. Lea M. McGee

Silly Millies and the Silly Millies logo are trademarks of
The Millbrook Press, Inc.

Published by The Millbrook Press, Inc.
2 Old New Milford Road
Brookfield, Connecticut 06804

Library of Congress Cataloging-in-Publication Data
Hayward, Linda.
It takes three / Linda Hayward ; illustrations by Robin Michal Koontz.
p. cm. — (Silly Millies)
Summary: Animals at the Compare-A-Thon compete to determine who
is the tallest, longest, slowest, largest, and fastest.
ISBN 0-7613-2902-1 (lib. bdg.) — ISBN 0-7613-1798-8 (pbk.)
[1. Animals—Fiction. 2. Comparison (Grammar)—Fiction. 3. Stories in
rhyme.] I. Koontz, Robin Michal, ill. II. Title. III. Series.
PZ8.3.H33384 It 2003 [E]—dc21 2002011410

# It Takes Three

The sun is up.

The race is on!

Let's go and see

Compare-A-Thon.

The race for TALL is at Tall Wall.

Let's cheer for Stork

6    for he is **tall**.

Let's cheer for Horse.

She is **taller** yet.

Just look how far up she can get! 7

But it takes three for us to say

who is the **tallest** one today.

Giraffe is it!

Let's cheer—

"HOORAY!"

We cheer, and yet he cannot hear.

His ears are just too far away.

9

The race for SLOW is the next show.

Who moved . . . and when . . .

is hard to know.

The Snail is **slow.**

She sets the pace.

But Slug is **slower** in this race.

Sponge is **slowest** of the three.

If Sponge has moved,

we did not see!

The race for LARGE is on a barge.

See Elephant.

Now he is **large**.

But look at this.

The water hid a **larger** beast—

the Giant Squid!

Blue Whale is the **largest**—YO!

Into the water we all go!

The race for SMALL is in Small Hall.

You must be near to see it all!

Goldfinch is here.
He sure is **small**.

The Hummingbird is **smaller** yet.

Two drops of rain will make him wet!

18

The Pygmy Shrew is very wee.

She is the **smallest** of the three.

The race for WIDE takes place outside.

See Flying Lemur.

He is **wide**.

The Flying Fox is in this set,

and she is even **wider** yet.

But not as wide as Albatross,
who is the **widest** one across!

The LONG Tongue Race is in this place.
When tongues unroll, they need some space!

Fruit Bat may win.
Her tongue is **long**.
"Go Bat!" we chant our Go-Bat song.

The reptile's tongue is **longer,** so we all chant, "Go, Chameleon, Go!"

Anteater has the **longest** flap.

Her tongue is just a sticky trap.

"Go Anteater!" we all chant.

All of us—except the Ant!

The race for ODD
is in P Pod.

Look at Mole Rat.

He is **odd**.

He has no hair, no neck, no snout.

His ears stick in instead of out!

The Platypus is **odder** yet.

Just how mixed-up can one beast get?

Duck feet . . . duck bill . . . and yet no quack.

She has a furry tail in back!

Porcupine Fish is here . . . beware!

He looks so cute but do take care.

Sharp spines around a silly face—

He is the **oddest** in this race.

Spines and fins and gills and all.

When he puffs up, he is a ball!

The race for FAST is here at last.

Well, it <u>was</u> here. . . .

It just went past!

There goes the Hound.

She can be **fast**.

There goes the Hare

right up the hill.

28    Just see how he is **faster** still.

But now we all just stand and stare
as Cheetah passes Hound <u>and</u> Hare.

Cheetah was the **fastest** one.

Now she can rest.

30    The race is done!

And so we come to Exit Bend.

Compare-A-Thon is at an end.

Cheers and waves and all the rest!

Everyone has done their best!

## Dear Parents:

Congratulations! By sharing this book with your child, you are taking an important step in helping him or her become a good reader. *It Takes Three* is perfect for the child who is beginning to read alone. Below are some ideas for making sure your child's reading experience is a positive one.

### Tips for Reading
- First, read the book aloud to your child. Then, if your child is able to "sound out" the words, invite him or her to read to you. If your child is unsure about a word, you can help by asking, "What word do you think it might be?" or, "Does that make sense?" Point to the first letter or two of the word and ask your child to make that sound. If she or he is stumped, read the word slowly, pointing to each letter as you sound it out. Always provide lots of praise for the hard work your child is doing.
- If your child knows the words but is having trouble reading aloud, cut a plain white ruler-sized strip of paper to place under the line as your child reads. This will help your child keep track of his or her place.
- If your child is a beginning reader, have her or him read this book aloud to you. Reading and rereading is the best way to help any child become a successful reader.

### Tips for Discussion
- *It Takes Three* is about making comparisons. Use this book to help children learn to use words that compare two things (tall/tall<u>er</u>) and three things (tall/tall<u>er</u>/tall<u>est</u>).
- As you read the book, ask your child questions: Which animal is taller? Tallest? Larger? Largest? Etc.
- Next, ask your child to make comparisons of familiar objects or family members. You can help by letting your child complete sentences that compare: "Mom is taller than _____, but Dad is _____."

**Lea M. McGee, Ed.D.**
**Professor, Literacy Education**
**University of Alabama**